Only God Can Make God Known

BRENDON NAICKER

Table of Contents

1. Introduction

So who was Jesus Christ? If you are offended that I posed the question in the past-tense - you can be rest assured that what Jesus Christ was He is, and what He is He was. So here is the logic, Colossians 1:16 states, *"For by him all things were created, in heaven and on earth, visible and invisible, whether thrones or dominions or rulers or authorities — all things were created through him and for him"*; and in Hebrews 13:8 it mentions that *"Jesus Christ is the same yesterday and today and forever."* Therefore, there are no impossibilities of time and space for what Jesus Christ was He is, and what He is, He was. In John 1:1, *"In the beginning was the Word, and the Word was with God, and the Word was God."*

Therefore, if Jesus Christ is the way, truth and the life then ultimately the fate and destination of every living and those dead all hang upon the answer to this question, "Who was Jesus Christ?" This question is by no means a new one - for the Old and New Testaments provide the truth spoken by the Prophets and the Apostles they all pointed to the paths of the two roads, that being the broad and the narrow. Thus, how we answer the question would also reflects our nature. In John 8:44 it states, *"You are of your father the devil, and your will is to do your father's desires. He was a murderer from the beginning, and does not stand in the truth, because there is no truth in him. When he lies, he speaks out of his own character, for he is a liar and the father of lies."*

"Many other signs therefore Jesus also performed in the presence of the disciples, which are not written in this book; but these have been written that you may believe that Jesus is the Christ, the Son of God; and that believing you may have life in His name" (John 20:30-31). The Apostle John wrote his gospel with the expressed intention of convincing his readers to believe in Jesus Christ and that Jesus Christ is the Son of God.

2. Whom do men say that I the Son of Man am?

In the first century, many Jews expected that when the Messiah came He would deliver them from the Roman oppression. In John 6:15, *"Perceiving then that they were about to come and take him by force to make him king, Jesus withdrew again to the mountain by himself."* The people were expecting a political Messiah, a lion of a character and not a lamb of one riding on a donkey.

It is very common to miss the Messiah when the human heart is set on things of this world. So possibly not realising that their real oppressor was sin and alienation from God, and not the physical temporal inconveniences of the Roman domination. However, the identity of Jesus Christ had become evident to those who encountered Him as in John 1:41, *"He first found his own brother Simon and said to him, "We have found the Messiah"* (which means Christ). In the presence of the Messiah we are only able to see the state of our being - within our nature when first coming to the awakening of who He is.

In Matthew 16:13 we read, *"Now when Jesus came into the district of Caesarea Philippi, he asked his disciples, "Who do people say that the Son of Man is?""* It was the Apostle Peter who answered this question correctly, and this not by knowledge acquired but a revelation as he affirmed in Matthew 16:16 – *"Simon Peter replied, "You are the Christ, the Son of the living God.""* In verse 17, *"and Jesus answered him, "Blessed are you, Simon Bar-Jonah! For flesh and blood have not revealed this to you, but my Father who is in heaven.""* One can only imagine being one of the disciples witnessing such profundity from plain-old Peter.

This must have been one of the memorable moments of Jesus' ministry. In these few words spoken by Peter echoing the voices of those long gone all looking in faith to that day, to which Peter is now beholding that which Abraham saw. In Matthew 22:41-46, a similar question is posed but this time it is answered in denial of the Messiah.

"Now while the Pharisees were gathered together, Jesus asked them a question, saying, "What do you think about the Christ? Whose son is he?" They said to him, "The son of David." He

said to them, "How is it then that David, in the Spirit, calls him Lord, saying,

"'The Lord said to my Lord,
"Sit at my right hand,
until I put your enemies under your feet"'?
If then David calls him Lord, how is he his son?" And no one was able to answer him a word, nor from that day did anyone dare to ask him any more questions."

Those who claimed to have known God and understand His words are now baffled and left speechless for their hearts now being exposed to the reality of their preconceived notions of how they saw the Messiah. Thus they were not willing to answer for this will be an affirmation of a divine human son of David, that being the Messiah.

People are still answering the question by conveniently "packaging" the Messiah so to conceal their true heart's condition - trying to bind-up the revelation of the Messiah just like those religious leaders of Jesus' day. For to acknowledge the Messiah as Jesus - would result in revealing who they are! As in the words of Jesus stated in Matthew 23:33, *"You serpents, you brood of vipers, how are you to escape being sentenced to hell?"* It is for this very reason that Jesus Christ is so humanised in our culture presenting Him as a weak and mild person whose life and work could never seriously affect much less change the course of history. This type of Jesus Christ is preached in many a dead church thus it produces no life nor offence - people like it because they can still be in control of their lives. In Matthew 10:22, we read *"...and you will be hated by all for my name's sake. But the one who endures to the end will be saved."* Is the message you are sharing causing people to hate you? Or is there another gospel?

3. They shall call His name Immanuel

Matthew 1:21-23, *"She will bear a son, and you shall call his name Jesus, for he will save his people from their sins." All this took place to fulfil what the Lord had spoken by the prophet: "Behold, the virgin shall conceive and bear a son, and they shall call his name Immanuel (which means, God with us)."*

There are many who would be willing to pay for getting their fortune read, and so eager are they to seek out their future. Yet the Bible is filled with extraordinary prophecies which even if one were intoxicated could not have concocted, however making it up is only half of the problem. How does one make prophecy come alive if it's not God ordained? As words don't have life in themselves. So just as King Saul sought his future from the dead we too are forced to look down into the pits of darkness when trying to seek the knowledge about ourselves outside of God. Regrettably it is from the dead and not from the heavens.

So when the Apostle Matthew mentions in Matthew 1:21-23, he is quoting a prophecy from the prophet Isaiah written in 700BC (before Christ incarnate). Is that not mind blowing? The prophecy states in Isaiah 7:14, *"Therefore the Lord himself will give you a sign. Behold, the virgin shall conceive and bear a son, and shall call his name Immanuel."*

This prophecy would need a miracle to be fulfilled for the supernatural sign of the virgin birth of the Messiah who would be called Immanuel or God with us. This would be the assurance Israel would see as a sign of the faithfulness of the Lord God to the Abrahamic promise. Thus Jesus Christ is shown to be very God of very God and with us. Therefore Matthew is affirming the full deity of Jesus of Nazareth, as he further elaborated on other prophecies such as Isaiah 8:8 and Isaiah 11:1-15. However an astounding verse in Isaiah 9:6 states,

> *"For to us a child is born,*
>
> *to us a son is given;*
>
> *and the government shall be upon his shoulder,*
>
> *and his name shall be called*
>
> *Wonderful Counsellor, Mighty God,*
>
> *Everlasting Father, Prince of Peace."*

4. Can we call Jesus God?

In John's gospel there are several texts that confirm who Jesus Christ was. The opening verses to John's gospel states, in John 1:1, *"In the beginning was the Word, and the Word was with God, and the Word was God."* This is a comparison to Genesis 1:1, *"In the beginning, God created the heavens and the earth."* The Apostle John is taking the reader back beyond creation. It states in effect at the time of creation the Word was already in existence. Thereby, *"In the beginning was the word"* highlights the eternity of the Word.

Just as fascinating to seeing how prophecy is fulfilled it is equally astonishing to see how heresies get repackaged and resurface like a plague whose only objective is to detour truth seekers. Arius of Alexandrian, a 4th Century heretic whose views were condemned at the Council of Nicaea in 325 A.D. said of Christ, "There was a time when he was not." The Council however, followed the Apostles' teaching - thereby denying Arius' views. That weed, however, has now grown into a bush, resurfacing in forms such as the Jehovah's

Witnesses and the Mormons who deny the eternality of Jesus Christ and the divine Trinity.

Second clause in John 1:1, *"and the Word was with God"* stresses the Son's community of unity within the Godhead. The words describe in brief the eternal communion of the Son and the Father. This is reaffirmed in John 1:18, *"No one has ever seen God; the only God, who is at the Father's side, he has made him known".*

Third clause, *"and the Word was God."* portrays the deity of the Word. Thus that the Word is classified as a divine being. By opening his gospel in this manner John wants us to read his gospel in the light of the deity of the Son.

His mighty signs and words as recorded in this gospel are the miracles and words of God. The Son is the eternal God, yet distinct from the Father in personality.

The Apostle John further goes on to mention in affirming the deity of Jesus Christ in John 1:18, *"No one has ever seen God; the only God, who is at the Father's side, he has made him known".* Thus showing oneness of essence between Father and Son. In addition, Apostle John mentions in John 10:30, *"I and the Father are one."* Thereby bearing upon the essential unity. It is interesting that whether the word *"one"* is neuter in gender, or literally, one thing. Thus implying that a deep unity is meant, and it certainly seems to mean more than oneness of will and that implication is that only God could say and guarantee these claims. For who could promise such as affirmed in the latter verses of John 10:27-30, *"My sheep hear my voice, and I know them, and they follow me. I give them eternal life, and they will never perish, and no one will snatch them out of my hand. My Father, who has given them to me, is greater than all, and no one is able to snatch them out of the Father's hand. I and the Father are one."*

In John 20:28, Thomas answered him, *"My Lord and my God!"* Here is a confession which there can be no doubt that it confirms the deity of Jesus Christ. This confession of faith that Jesus Christ is God was uttered publicly from a reaction not out of belief or doctrine but a heart which had been moved. We all had learnt in Sunday School of "doubting Thomas" and how we are to have faith. However contrary to popular belief, Thomas was no skeptic for he valiantly suggested in John 11:16, *"So Thomas, called the Twin, said to his fellow disciples, "Let us also go, that we may die with him.""* The

Apostle John must have agreed with this confession about Christ's deity for the John cites Thomas' confession at the climax of the argument of the gospel.

5. Jesus was in the form of God

Philippians 2:6 states, *"(Jesus,) who, though he was in the form of God, did not count equality with God a thing to be grasped."* The theological term referring to the union of the two natures in one person as the "hypostatic union". Thereby the Apostle Paul notes that Jesus was in the form of God - this term, *form* - in the Greek original, refers to the *unchangeable essential nature of a thing*. For example, if we are to say that a person is in the form of man then what was meant was that he had the essential nature of manhood. So an orange, apple, banana, etc. all have the same form being fruits, but they have different outward characteristics.

If Jesus is in the form of God, then He has all the essential attributes of deity, or all those characterising qualities that make God. Thereby, Jesus is in the form of God is God. Paul is merely stating that Jesus did not surrender His divine attributes but chose voluntarily not to use them or to set them aside. Hence surrendering the glory, majesty, and the prerogatives of deity, but not the deity itself.

6. Our great God and Saviour Jesus Christ

Titus 2:13-14 states, *"waiting for our blessed hope, the appearing of the glory of our great God and Saviour Jesus Christ, who gave himself for us to redeem us from all lawlessness and to purify for himself a people for his own possession who are zealous for good works."* There is no mincing of words here for it is clearly written that our Saviour Jesus Christ is God. So in "waiting for that blessed hope" - is "the glorious appearing of the great God and our Saviour Jesus Christ", affirms Apostle Paul. This is not the only Scripture which refers to Jesus Christ as God for we can look at Hebrews 1:8 and 2 Peter 1:1 for in both these passages Jesus Christ is also affirmed as God. Therefore to deny the deity of Jesus Christ would be heresy. The evidence is that the Son, Jesus Christ possesses undiminished deity.

7. Only God can make God known

Jesus Christ is the revealer of God in John 1:18, it states that, *"No one has ever seen God; the only God, who is at the Father's side, he has made him known."* Jesus is the Messiah, He is the knowledge of God manifested to mankind, He is the only unique Son, eternally resting upon the side of the Father, in communion.

Therefore Apostle John would state in John 1:14, *"And the Word became flesh and dwelt among us, and we have seen his glory, glory as of the only Son from the Father, full of grace and truth."* So when Phillip requested to see the Father, Jesus responded in John 14:8-10, *"Philip said to him, "Lord, show us the Father, and it is enough for us."* Jesus said to him, *"Have I been with you so long, and you still do not know me, Philip? Whoever has seen me has seen the Father. How can you say, "Show us the Father?" Do you not believe that I am in the Father and the Father is in me? The words that I say to you I do not speak on my own authority, but the Father who dwells in me does his works.""* Augustine of Hippo rightly stated that, "It is through the man Christ that you proceed to the God Christ."

8. Jesus Christ is the I AM

Many Christians recognise that Jesus applied the Name of Jehovah to Himself by the way He said *"I Am"*. In Greek, one can say *"I am"* by using a single word, *"eimi"* without a pronoun. The Name *"I AM"* is two words, *"ego eimi"* with the pronoun added. God said to Moses, *"I AM WHO I AM."* This is what you are to say to the Israelites, *"I AM has sent me to you."* (Exodus 3:14).

In Isaiah 41:4 and 45:18 the LORD refers to Himself as I AM. Note that Scripture never states Jesus as saying *"I am God"*. If it had, that would not be as strong as His confessing of the divine Name by simply saying, *"I Am"*!

So what we do see is that Jesus used, *"I Am"* with both Greek words to refer to Himself numerous times. One of the most astonishing moment was when He stated in John 8:58-59, *""Truly, truly," Jesus answered, "before Abraham was born, I am!" At this, they picked up stones to stone him…"* This was a claim of pre-existence. It fits in well with His repeated claim that He had come from above mentioned in John 6:33, 38, 50, 51, 58.

Jesus' clearest word in John 8:58, is that all that the LORD of the Old Testament is thus applies fully to Him. His contemporaries knew instantly that He had taken the Lord's Name as His own. He was saying that He was the LORD God of Abraham and the Messiah Abraham was waiting for. That is why those listening wanted to stone him for blasphemy.

9. Jesus is the sustainer

This should affect our reading of the other *I Am's* in the Gospel of John such as in, 6:35; 8:12; 10:7; 10:11; 11:25; 14:6; and 15:1. In addition, Jesus was also saying I am something for these *"I AM's"* that being; the Bread of Life; the Good Shepherd; the Resurrection and the Life; the Way, the Truth and the Life; and the True Vine through whom life flows – how could anyone be such things without being the ultimate giver and sustainer of life? In other words, how could Jesus be such things without being God Himself? He made this known about Himself by combining the "I Am" Name with abilities only God has.

10. Works that no one else did

So for God to reveal God there should be verifying evidences which provide witness to His deity. Miracles performed by Jesus Christ testify of His deity but Prophets and Apostles also performed miracles and deity is not claimed for them. The differences are evident that when Christ spoke it was unlike any man had spoken before, for His words were of sovereign authority. This can be seen in the miracles from the Gospel accounts such as demons submitting to His authority, the controlling of the raging water of the storm in the Sea of Galilee, the forgiving of sinners, and the authority of His mere word spoken which transcended distance for the healing of centurion's servant.

The words of Jesus Christ were definitely potent of processing that of life and death - the cursing of the fig tree and the raising of Lazarus from the dead are similar to that of Genesis, *"Let there be light and there was light."* The works of Jesus Christ's were by the power of God. Jesus had a complete and continuous communion and dependence on His Father, which is itself a witness to the fact that He, although a man, is more than a man.

At the stilling of the storm, Mark describes the once storm which they feared for their lives to it obeying the words of Jesus Christ. Mark 4:41 states, *"And they were filled with great fear and said to one another, "Who then is this, that even the wind and the sea obey him?"*

Another instance was on the Sea of Galilee where Peter and his crew had toiled all night without a catch - that Jesus upon the land is able to perform the miracle of the mighty haul of fish caught. I love how the Scriptures describe the event, *"when the weight of the fish became so great that the boats began to sink."* In Luke 5:8 records the words of Peter becoming so overwhelmed with conviction that he fell to his knees crying out, *"depart from me for I am a sinful man, oh Lord."*

Therefore the witnesses of Jesus Christ's works of the supernatural were indeed out of this World. Hence in John 15:24, *"If I had not done among them the works that no one else did, they would not be guilty of sin, but now they have seen and hated both me and my Father."*

11. Words that no one else spoke

Words spoken by Jesus Christ set Him apart as the supreme and unique revealer of truth for no one else spoke like He did. The greatest of the Prophets of the Old Testament would usually begin a prophecy by stating, *"Thus sayeth the Lord"* but Jesus Christ characteristically prefaced His with, *"Verily I say unto you."* The use of verily shows a finality and authority in His message. It is for this reason we read in Matthew 7:28-29, *"And when Jesus finished these sayings, the crowds were astonished at his teaching for he was teaching them as one who had authority, and not as their scribes."* This accounts for the officer's words in John 7:46, *"The officers answered, "No one ever spoke like this man!"*

The fathers and prophets of the past spoke but it is Jesus Christ who has the final word noted at *"spoken".* In Hebrews 1:1-2 it states that, *"Long ago, at many times and in many ways, God spoke to our fathers by the prophets but in these last days he has spoken to us by his Son, whom he appointed the heir of all things, through whom also he created the world."* Jesus Christ is the truth and the life. Both God's truth and God's way are embodied in Jesus Christ.

12. Walk that no one else calls

Jesus says to His disciples, *"Follow me."* In all the religions and philosophies of the world, a follower can follow the teachings of its founder. However this is not the same for Jesus Christ as He cannot be separated from His teachings. Aristotle said to his disciples, "follow my teachings." Socrates likewise said to his disciples to follow his teachings. Confucius said to his disciples to follow his sayings. Buddha said to his disciples to follow his mediations, and Muhammad said to his disciples to follow his noble pillars. But it is only Jesus who says to His followers to deny themselves, take up their cross and follow Him.

The biggest difference is that Christ is still alive and He embodies His teachings. All the other founders of religions do not require a relationship with its leaders however this is not the case with Jesus Christ. For to those who are not following Jesus Christ the Apostle Matthew explains in Matthew 10:32-33, *"So everyone who acknowledges me before men, I also will acknowledge before my Father who is in heaven, but whoever denies me before men, I also will deny before my Father who is in heaven."*

13. Power to forgive sins

The forgiveness of sins is the prerogative of God and God alone. Therefore it was unthinkable for anyone listening to Jesus Christ forgiving the sins of the man with paralysis in Mark 2:1-12. When Jesus saw the faith of the men going to such great extents to reach out to Jesus for their friend's healing. He said to one who was paralysed, *"Son, your sins are forgiven"*. Now the religious leaders sitting there and reasoning in their hearts as this sounded like blaspheme. Jesus responds to them, *"Which is easier, to say to the paralytic, "Your sins are forgiven", or to say, "Rise, take up your bed and walk?""*

How does one see the empirical proof of forgiveness of sins for this functions in the realm beyond the sphere of human observation and verification? For if Jesus Christ had been lying then God would not honour the words of a lying man. If the words, *"you are forgiven"* did take effect in the invisible world then this magnificent demonstration of power is a result of the declaration that God had forgiven. But Jesus did not say this for He claimed that He had the authority and power to forgive sins. Thus in the natural sense of His words Jesus has the authority to forgive sins which rested in His own person because He is God. As affirmed in Mark 2:10, *" "But that you may know that the Son of Man has authority on earth to forgive sins "— he said to the paralytic. "*

14. Jesus accepts worship

In Exodus 20:3-4, *"You shall have no other gods before me. You shall not make for yourself a carved image, or any likeness of anything that is in heaven above, or that is in the earth beneath, or that is in the water under the earth.* Scripture affirms that we do not worship that which is not the LORD God. We also witness instances when men are requested not to bow down to angels. However we see that Jesus received and accepted the worship of people. It would be inconceivable that Jesus should accept such worship if He were not in reality worthy of it. Let's see how the Apostle John in Revelation 22:8-9 responds, *"I, John, am the one who heard and saw these things. And when I heard and saw them, I fell down to worship at the feet of the angel who showed them to me, but he said to me, "You must not do that! I am a fellow servant with you and your brothers the prophets, and with those who keep the words of this book. Worship God."*

Note that the angel tells John not to worship him but to worship God. However in Chapters 4 and 5, it is seen that the worship of the Lamb of God, the Lord Jesus Christ - implying that Jesus Christ is God and is worthy of worship.

In the Book of Revelation the vision of the throne of God the Father and of the lion of the tribe of Judah, the Lamb of God reaches its climax with the declaration that the Lamb has finished the work of redemption that restores world dominion to Him and His redeemed people. All heaven, it seems, the four beasts, the twenty-four elders, myriads of angels, in fact every creature in heaven and on earth and under the earth and in the sea, and all that is in them, proclaim the praises of the Lamb. John concludes the account with the words, *""To him who sits on the throne and to the Lamb be blessing and honor and glory and might forever and ever!" And the four living creatures said, "Amen!" and the elders fell down and worshiped."*

15. Word became flesh

In John 1:14, *"And the Word became flesh and dwelt among us, and we have seen his glory, glory as of the only Son from the Father, full of grace and truth."* The word, *"Word"*, referred in John 1:14 is the Greek word *"logos"*, it is a term for the person of Christ. Thus having been assumed into union with the logos, it was miraculously sanctified so as to be sinless and perfect.

Jesus Christ was truly the son of Mary, but at the same time He was also the sinless Son of God. The result of the incarnation, the conception and the incarnation were that Jesus Christ was *"bone of her bone and flesh of her flesh"* of her substance. Mary was the mother of Jesus' human soul as well as of his human body, the two natures in Jesus Christ that proceeded from the time of the embryo on through into the time of His manhood.

"And the Word became flesh" let us look at this in light of John 1:1, *"In the beginning was the Word"*. That Word is God predestined to speak to men. So divine Word has taken on

human form. Therefore in becoming flesh the Word does not cease to be the divine Word.

The term flesh in *"He became flesh"* is referring to human nature. The immutability of the Son as well as His deity are not compromised by this term, for the being of the Word does not have a new existence. However He does, with the assumption of a human nature in addition to His divine nature, thus entering into a new form of existence.

In John 1, *"The Word was"* which is in juxtaposition with verse 14, *"The Word became"*. In verse 1 we read that, *"The Word was God"* while in verse 14, we have *"The Word became flesh"*. The eternal being stands in contrast with the temporal becoming of the God Son becoming man.

In verse 1, we read that, *"The Word was with God"* while in verse 14, *"the Word came to be with us."* In verse 1, we have, *"The Word was God,"* while in verse 14, we have *"The Word became flesh."* The eternal being stands in contrast with the temporal becoming of the God Son. Thereby then in John 1:14 states that the divine Son became man.

16. Jesus is sinless

In 2 Corinthians 5:21 notes, *"For our sake he made him to be sin who knew no sin, so that in him we might become the righteousness of God."* This verse illustrates the sinlessness of Jesus Christ. Take note of the word, *"knew"* for it expresses personal experience. Hence, the expression, *"who knew no sin"* stresses the fact that Jesus Christ had no personal participation, no experience of sin.

The Apostle Peter affirms this in 1 Peter 2:22, *"He committed no sin, neither was deceit found in his mouth."* Apostle John concurs, in 1 John 3:5 he states, *"You know that he appeared in order to take away sins, and in him there is no sin."* The Apostle Paul stated that we *"all"* have sinned thus every person is naturally born in sin and lawless - but it is only Jesus Christ who is sinless and was manifested to take away sins. Therefore *"Jesus knew no sin"* - He did no sin, and in Him there was no sin.

17. Jesus' humanity

The great *"I AM"*, where no name could ever be appropriate to the eternal God takes on a human name. In Matthew 1, the author in setting out his genealogy writes, *"The book of the generations of Jesus Christ, the son of David, the son of Abraham"*. Later an angel of the Lord instructs Joseph to give the Son the name Jesus, a human name, the Greek equivalent of the Old Testament name of Joshua.

In 1 Timothy 2:5, Apostle Paul writes, *"For there is one God, and there is one mediator between God and men, the man Christ Jesus"*. This is an attribute of the Messiah to the title of the Messiah with humanity. For in Matthew 1:1-17, we read of the genealogy of Jesus Christ traced down through David and Abraham. In verse 25, we read that Mary gave birth to Jesus Christ. Thus the description of the conception and birth describes it as a human through miraculous conception as in Luke 1:35, *"And the angel answered her, "The Holy Spirit will come upon you, and the power of the Most High will overshadow you; therefore the child to be born will be called holy—the Son of God.""*

We must remember that Jesus was not a mere spirit being in some figment of someone's imagination for He had constituent parts of a human personality and anatomy. He is said to have a body, soul, and spirit. In addition we find through the gospel accounts that He exercised human emotions, getting angry at unrighteousness and being sorrowful. He showed having physical wants of being hungry, thirsty, and falling asleep. Hanging upon that cross many had seen Him suffering - human suffering and death.

It is clear that the Bible portrays Jesus Christ as both God and man. Jesus Christ was different to man as in that He had a supernatural conception as affirmed in Luke 1:35. He was conceived of the Holy Spirit, born of the Virgin Mary. He was the sinless Son of God. Jesus assumed an impersonal human nature. His personality was His divine and eternal personality, His two natures being united in one undivided and indivisible person. The human nature was received into the person of the *logos*.

To sum up Jesus' make up would be that He is not God in dwelling, nor man raised to the power of deity but the God-man. *"For in him the whole fullness of deity dwells bodily."* Thus Jesus is not God in Man, nor God and Man, but one person, the God-Man.

In Philippians 2:6-8 Apostle Paul confesses the full and complete humanity of Jesus Christ *"who, though he was in the form of God, did not count equality with God a thing to be grasped, but emptied himself, by taking the form of a servant, being born in the likeness of men. And being found in human form, he humbled himself by becoming obedient to the point of death, even death on a cross."*

Hebrews 2:14 states, *"Since therefore the children share in flesh and blood, he himself likewise partook of the same things, that through death he might destroy the one who has the power of death, that is, the devil."* The two verbs represent the concept of sharing in the verse. The first word *"share"* suggests the idea in common and yields and emphasis upon the sharing in a common nature that human beings possess. The tense of the verb suggests that they have always shared these common qualities.

The second verb, rendered by *"partook"* referring to Jesus Christ incarnation suggests that the nature He took was an additional nature for Him. It is that with which by nature He had nothing in common until the incarnation for He was the eternal Son. The tense underlines the historicity of the assumption of the nature that Jesus Christ betrothed Himself to the human race for better, for worse forever.

So, in Hebrews 2:17 it states, *"Therefore he had to be made like his brothers in every respect, so that he might become a merciful and faithful high priest in the service of God, to make propitiation for the sins of the people."* Christ is not two but one, that not by conversion of the God-head into flesh but by taking of the manhood into God.

18. Who is this at Lazarus' tomb?

We read that *"Jesus wept"*. This is Jesus the man. Then we read John 11:43 that Jesus *"cried out with a loud voice, "Lazarus come out.""* And the man who had died for four days came out from the dead. This is Jesus Christ the God-man.

19. Jesus is physically alive

The bodily resurrection of Jesus Christ is unique and it is essential to the Christian faith for when Jesus was raised from the dead - He was raised to die no more. There have been no others who have died and later seen resurrected witnessed by more than five hundred people. In the accounts of the life of Buddha there is no claim to resurrection. However it is mentioned that at the dead of Buddha it was noted, "that utter passing away in which nothing whatever remains behind". Muhammed died on 8th June 632 A.D, and there is no claim to his resurrection. However the dust of Muhammad's remains are located in Medina. Therefore the bodily resurrection is unique to Christianity.

If Jesus Christ was merely a man and concocted some theories and philosophies. If He had just provided some teachings about God - then it would have made no difference considering His bodily remains on earth would have shown Him to have not testified to His teachings. Remember Jesus Christ pronouncing that He was the resurrection and the life and He said that He was the one that, if we believed in Him, He would give life to all those who do believe.

How tragic and devastating it would be if Jesus had not resurrected from the dead. However that's how the disciples did feel, for it was the women that went out that morning, feeling of grief and hopelessness must have filled their hearts for their Lord was put to death and assumed that their cause to follow Him was now over for He was defeated.

Their concerns were as to who's going to roll away the stone for us from the tomb? They wanted to serve the dying body but to their shock - they didn't expect to find the resurrected Saviour Jesus Christ. Scripture described them as being so excited and shocked, became so fearful, that *"they fled in terror."*

Many of us would like to serve the dead, the defeated Jesus in the tomb. We have very little hope in His words to expect miracles or believe what He said that He will do. Just like the Sanhedrin, we do not deny the empty tomb, we just want to be able to explain it in a different way that is convincing to the natural mind. There are many theories attempting to deny the bodily resurrection of Jesus Christ so to comfort and conceal the spiritual death of our lives. However what if Jesus is who He says He is? For the natural-man would rather have a body like other religions of the world. Thus believing in a subjective belief which has no absolute truth offends no one.

However Jesus Christ claimed exclusivity being *"the only way, truth and the life"*. In Him is the only light for the lost world and that all men are in darkness so apart from Him there is no truth or life. Obviously we can't have that, considering it exposes our depravity and the state of being, living outside of truth. So we make-up reasons for why there isn't a body in the tomb rather than the possibility of believing that there is a spiritual dimension which exists outside of our control. The most bewildering aspect of all this is seeing the material world being overcome by the spiritual and darkness could not put it out.

Let me explain, we place so much of our faith in that which we can see and touch - we call this our reality. So Jesus comes to this world (the one He created) and dies just like any man. His body laid dead, and would and should decompose like everyone else but this is when the Son of Man manifests being the Son of God to transform even the earthly material body to a glorified being, able to walk through doors like a spirit and eat food which is material? The resurrection body of Jesus possessed capabilities which enabled Him to pass through that which is material.

20. The grave clothes

In John 20:4-8 it states, *"Both of them were running together, but the other disciple outran Peter and reached the tomb first. And stooping to look in, he saw the linen cloths lying there, but he did not go in. Then Simon Peter came, following him, and went into the tomb. He saw the linen cloths lying there, and the face cloth, which had been on Jesus' head, not lying with the linen cloths but folded up in a place by itself. Then the other disciple, who had reached the tomb first, also went in, and **he saw and believed.**"*

The Apostle John states that the grave clothes were arranged in a manner which implied that Jesus Christ had risen from the dead. Jesus had told them about this in John 20:9, but they did not understand, *"for as yet they did not understand the Scripture, that he must rise from the dead."* However when the Apostle John saw the grave clothes, *"he saw and believed"*. The stone being rolled away was not so that Jesus could leave the tomb through the opening. It was to be a witness so that others might see and believe. The stone was not removed to let Jesus Christ out of the tomb, but it was to let others in to see into the tomb that He had been raised. The Apostle John in seeing the clothes and believing came to a spiritual perception to Him that Jesus Christ had been raised from the dead.

21. Importance of the resurrection

The resurrection is the proof of the defeat of death and of the offences and He was raised again on account of our justification. The resurrection of Jesus Christ is the evidence from God that the cross of Jesus Christ is sufficient to pay for our sins. It is the proof of the forgiveness of sins. It is the proof of the defeat of death. Thus, we gaze upon that cross of Jesus Christ, we see the atonement made and so we are reunited with our Creator. When looking at the resurrection of Jesus Christ we see the atonement accepted. Thereby uniting the church to Himself. Jesus did not raise himself from the dead but the Scriptures are clear it was the Holy Spirit who raised Jesus because the aim of this testimony is to get over to us the fact that the Father has accepted the work of the Son.

22. Jesus of Nazareth?

For hundreds of years, Christians have answered that He is God's Son, fully God, and also fully man. The classic formulation is found in the Nicene Creed (325 CE), which affirms that he is *"of the essence of the Father, God of God, Light of Light, very God of very God, begotten, not made, being of one substance with the Father."* The creed goes on to explain that he *"came down and was incarnate and was made man."* Much of what the Gospels have to say about Jesus has to do with questions such as *"Are you the Messiah"* as in Mark 14:61 and *"Who is this Son of Man?"* as in John 12:34.

23. The Messiah

The evangelists explain that Jesus sometimes conformed to people's expectations and that He sometimes corrected them. For instance in Matthew 2:3-6, the scribes were correct in predicting the birthplace of the Messiah. However in Luke 24:25-27, Jesus' disciples were unprepared for the fact that the Messiah had to suffer and die.

Therefore it is important to understand the expectations of Jewish people in looking towards the Messiah.

24. Contextualising

It is important to read the Bible within its historical context. We are so prone to contextualising the Scriptures by our own biases and presuppositions. This becomes particularly difficult when it comes to what the New Testament tells us about Jesus. We all think we know what it means when we read that Jesus is the Messiah, the Son of God, Lord, and Saviour. However the reality is that we have 2,000 years of Christian tradition that has taught us to understand these terms in a certain way, influenced by dogma and experiences.

Our presumption is that the Jews have had an idea of what the Messiah would resemble, but that was not the case. The reality was that many Jews in the first century would probably have said that they didn't know they were supposed to be waiting for the Messiah, and those who were waiting did not agree about what they were waiting for. For in Luke 11:52, we see that just like our day - the religious leaders are merely religious having no life in faith, misguiding the flock. *"What sorrow awaits you experts in religious law! For you remove the key to knowledge from the people. You don't enter the Kingdom yourselves, and you prevent others from entering."*

25. What do we mean?

The English word *"Christ"* comes from the Greek *"christos"*, which is a translation of the Hebrew *"mashiach"*, a word that also has become the English term *"Messiah."*

"Messiah" or mashiach means the anointed one. Anointing with oil symbolised holiness. The anointed one was made holy and set apart for God as in Exodus 30:25-29, In 1 Samuel 9:16 we see the word used, *"Tomorrow about this time I will send to you a man from the land of Benjamin, and you shall anoint him to be prince over my people Israel. He shall save my people from the hand of the Philistines. For I have seen my people, because their cry has come to me."* We see Jesus Christ quoting Isaiah 61:1,

> *"The Spirit of the Lord GOD is upon me,*
> *because the LORD has anointed me*
> *to bring good news to the poor;*
> *he has sent me to bind up the brokenhearted,*
> *to proclaim liberty to the captives,*
> *and the opening of the prison to those who are bound".*

In summary we see the word used in the following ways: As kings (1 Samuel 10:1; 16:13 etc.), priests (Exodus 28:41; 1 Chronicles 29:22), and prophets (1 Kings 19:16; 1 Chronicles 16:22; Psalms 105:15) were anointed, they might all be called messiah. In an eschatological context, however, the word "messiah" (*mashiach*) occurs only twice, in Daniel 9:25-26, which refers to "the time of an anointed (*mashiach*) prince", and to "an anointed one (*mashiach*)" that will be cut off.

Biblical scholars agree that Jewish expectations of a Messiah are rooted in God's promise to David, which is recorded in both 2 Samuel 7:8-16, and in 1 Chronicles 17:7-14:1. In several Old Testament texts, this promise was applied to the king on Israel's throne. However some texts also look to the future for its fulfilment. A few later Jewish texts connect the promise with an eschatological character. Therefore to define the term "Messiah" as an eschatological figure that is understood as a fulfilment of God's promise to David. The part of the promise that specifically concerns offspring for David reads as follows: 2 Samuel 7:12-16

"...from the time that I appointed judges over my people Israel. And I will give you rest from all your enemies. Moreover, the LORD declares to you that the LORD will make you a house.

When your days are fulfilled and you lie down with your fathers, I will raise up your offspring after you, who shall come from your body, and I will establish his kingdom. 13 He shall build a house for my name, and I will establish the throne of his kingdom forever. 14 I will be to him a father, and he shall be to me a son. When he commits iniquity, I will discipline him with the rod of men, with the stripes of the sons of men, 15 but my steadfast love will not depart from him, as I took it from Saul, whom I put away from before you. 16 And your house and your kingdom shall be made sure forever before me. Your throne shall be established forever."

26. Definition of 2 Samuel 7:11-16

The house that God will build as in 2 Samuel 7 verse 11 which does not refer to a physical house but to a family. More specifically, it refers to a line of successors to David's throne – *a dynasty*. The promise appeared to have been fulfilled in David's son, Solomon, who built a temple for the Lord as in verse 13. *"To him"*, God promises a very special status. God *"will be a father to him, and he shall be a son to"* in verse 14. The function of the term *"son of God"* is to assure that the king rules by divine decree. It also describes a relationship of exceptional intimacy. Therefore the Messiah would be a human being with a special relationship to God. He would be exceptionally wise and righteous, and therefore pre-eminently qualified to serve as Israel's king, bring the people back to God, and restore their destiny. In the process, He would make the nations subject to Israel and their God. Scholars believe that there is no evidence that Jews in the first century believed the Messiah would be equal to God.

This is the very reason that the first century Jews missed the Messiah, they had been so fixated with the law and piousness that they lost the very meaning it served to fulfil. Some however such as Simeon who was able to identify the Messiah as an infant. *"He took him up in his arms and blessed God and said, "Lord, now you are letting your servant depart in peace, according to your word; for my eyes have seen your salvation that you have prepared in the presence of all peoples, a light for revelation to the Gentiles, and for glory to your people Israel.""* (Luke 2:28–32) Having seen the messiah, Simeon is now prepared to die.

Having all the learning and keeping all the rituals yet the majority were blinded to the purposes of God because they were too busy fulfilling their ambitions. In Hebrews 8:5-7, *"They serve a copy and shadow of the heavenly things. For when Moses was about to erect the tent, he was instructed by God, saying, "See that you make everything according to the pattern that was shown you on the mountain." But as it is, Christ has obtained a ministry that is as much more excellent than the old as the covenant he mediates is better, since it is enacted on better promises. For if that first covenant had been faultless, there would have been no occasion to look for a second."*

The Jews were so close to God yet so far from knowing Him, they worshipped the right God but sadly in their minds and hearts they were devoted to another. Many today are in similar predicaments, some have all Word and claim to know God but knowledge can't replace relationship. Then there are the second camp who claim to have relationship with God but are without knowledge of who He is and are experienced driven. It's not by might, nor by power and therefore as New Testament Christians it has to be a Holy Spirit led life of denying ourselves and taking up our cross and living the life in the flesh - in Christ!

27. The wonderful Good News

The Son took man's nature in the womb of Virgin Mary of her substance so that two whole and perfect natures, that is to say the Godhead and manhood were joined together in one person never to be divided. Man is distanced from God by sin. He is ignorant of God through sin. He is unlike God being in sin. So the glory of the gospel of Jesus Christ, the God-man and His atonement in mediatorial work is that God finds himself in this person and is with men, for He is man. And man finds himself in this person and he is with God, thus he who was distanced from God by sin is restored to God through sin comes to the knowledge of God through Christ and he who was unlike God in sin shall come to be like him in Christ.

28. Heretical understandings

Jesus Christ did warn the Church in Matthew 24:4-5, *"And Jesus answered them, "See that no one leads you astray. For many will come in my name, saying, 'I am the Christ,' and they will lead many astray."* Solomon was right when he wrote in Ecclesiastes 1:9, *"there is nothing new under the sun."* Whether it is to the true doctrine of God, as well as to heresy. There are no "new" heresies, just repackaged old theories that were refuted 2,000 years ago. Therefore when we hear of a "new revelation" the Christian needs to be diligent in ensuring that "new" does not add to Scripture or add to the finished work of Jesus Christ nor diminishes who Christ is within the Trinity. Here are some ancient heresies which were refuted by the early Church and we too should be vigilant to the devil's schemes.

Docetists it declared that the Lord Jesus Christ was perfect in man-ness, truly man, consubstantial with us (*homoousion*, not *homoiousion*, i.e. he is not of *"like* substance or being" with us, but he is "of the *same* substance" with us) according to man-ness, and born of Mary. They denied the humanity of Jesus, He only appeared to be human.

Samosatian adoptionists it insisted upon the personal subsistence of the Logos "begotten of the Father before the ages." They denied the deity of Jesus, but claim that at some point in His life He was "adopted" by God to this unique role of divine sonship.

Sabellians it distinguished the Son from the Father both by the titles of "Father" and "Son" and by its reference to the Father having begotten the Son before all ages. They denied the unique Person of Jesus as the second Person of the Trinity (in speaking of Jesus Christ, the orthodox position is "one Person, two natures"; in speaking of the Trinity, the orthodox position is that "there is one God, God eternally exists as three Persons – Father, Son and Holy Spirit – each Person is fully God").

Arians it affirmed that the Lord Jesus Christ was perfect in deity, truly God, and consubstantial with the Father (*homoousion*, not *homoiousion*, i.e. he is not of "*like* substance or being" with the Father, but he is "of the *same* substance" with the Father). (An earlier version of this was known as **Ebionism.**). They denied the deity of Jesus, though he is the greatest of created beings concluding this would be polytheistic.

Apollinarians, who had reduced Jesus' manness to a body and an "animal soul" (*psyche alogos*), it declared that Jesus had a "rational soul" (*psyche logike*), that is, a "spirit." They denied the full humanity of Jesus, concluding Jesus had a human body but a divine mind and spirit.

Nestorians it both described Mary as *theotokos*, i.e. the God-bearer (not *Christotokos*, i.e. the Christ bearer, emphasising that Mary bore the man Jesus, undermining that she actually bore the God-man Jesus) not in order to exalt Mary in the slightest, but in order to affirm Jesus 'true deity and the fact of a real incarnation, and spoke throughout of one and the same Son and one person and one subsistence, not parted or divided into two persons and whose natures are *in union* without division and without separation. They denied that Jesus is one Person, concluding He consisted of two separate persons, human and divine.

Eutychians it confessed that in Christ were two natures without confusion and without change, the property of each nature being preserved and concurring in the one person. They denied that Jesus had two natures, concluding that the human nature was absorbed by the divine nature, thus creating a third kind of nature.

Printed in Great Britain
by Amazon